BUGS—BIG
and Little

BUGS

BIG
and Little

by Alice L. Hopf

Illustrated with photographs

Julian Messner Ⓜ New York

Published by Julian Messner, a Simon &
Schuster Division of Gulf & Western
Corporation, Simon & Schuster Building,
1230 Avenue of the Americas, New York, N.Y.
10020.

JULIAN MESSNER and colophon are trade-
marks of Simon & Schuster, registered in the
U.S. Patent and Trademark Office.

Manufactured in the United States of America

Design by Philip Jaget

Library of Congress Cataloging in Publication Data
Hopf, Alice Lightner
    Bugs, big and little.

    Includes index.
    SUMMARY: Explains what insects are, examines some
interesting facts about them, and discusses collecting
and displaying them in the home or classroom.
      1. Insects—Juvenile literature. [1. Insects]
I. Title.
QL467.2.H66   595.7   80-20705
ISBN 0-671-34014-X

For Alice Gray

Long-time friend and mentor in the realms of entomology

PICTURE CREDITS

Contents

Bugs are Insects are . . .

How do you know an insect when you see it? One way is to count legs. All insects have six legs—when they are fully grown. Caterpillars, which are young butterflies and moths, have many legs. But when they grow up and become butterflies, they, too, have only six legs. A few butterflies seem to have only four legs. This is because they no longer use the front pair, which have become dried up and useless. If you look closely, you can see them folded against their chests.

Another way to know if you are looking at an insect is to see if they have antennae. *Antennae* (an-TEN-ee) are wire-like growths on the head of the insect. All insects have two antennae on the front of their heads. These are for feeling and smelling.

Insects have a hard, bone-like shell, which is their skeleton. The skeleton is on the outside of insects instead of inside, like ours. For this reason, an insect must shed its skeleton as it grows. A baby insect eats and eats until its shell, which is like a skin, is too tight. Underneath the old shell is a new and larger one waiting. When the tight skin bursts, the new skin

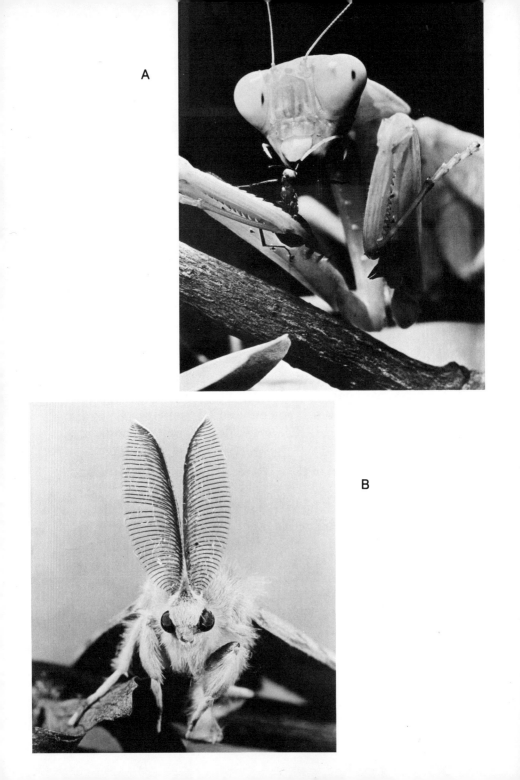

C

Different kinds of antennae. A. belongs to a praying mantis.
B. belongs to a male gypsy moth. C. are the antennae of a winged aphid.

underneath unfolds. The baby insect grows until it also fills that skin. Most insects shed their skins four to seven times before they are fully grown.

Insects grow in three different ways. The simplest hatch from the egg as tiny copies of their parents. Some insects are a little different from their parents when they hatch from the egg. They may not have the wings their parents have. They may be different in other ways. But by the time they are fully grown, they will be like their parents, wings and all.

The third kind of insect is born with an entirely different form from the parents. These babies are called *larvae* (LAR-vee). One is called a *larva*. Larvae are usually like little worms. Sometimes they have legs, and sometimes they are without. Caterpillars are the larvae of the butterfly or moth. They usually have legs and crawl about. Bee larvae have no legs. They spend all their time in cradle cells of the bees' comb and are fed by adult bees. All insects of this group have a third stage of growing which the first two groups do not have. The larvae turn into a form with a closed shell, called a *pupa*, usually without eyes or mouth or legs. Two or more are called *pupae* (pronounced PEW-pee). The little insect rests in the pupa and changes into adult form. When it comes out, it is a full-grown insect: a butterfly, a bee or an ant.

Insects hide from their enemies. This means you. It also means birds and animals and other insects. Insects also hide to catch other insects for a meal.

Some insects hide themselves by their color. A moth sitting

A

B

C

In picture A., a pupa
bursts its shell.
Pictures B. and C. show
it coming out as an
adult insect.

on the trunk of a tree has the same color as the tree. Some hide by looking like something else. They may have lines on their wings that are like the lines of the tree's bark. There is an insect called a walking stick that looks just like a stick. You might not notice it unless you saw it move. Some insects even have wings that look like leaves.

There is another insect called an ant lion that digs a pit and hides under the sand at the bottom, waiting for a meal. An ant may slip over the edge of the pit. It slides down the sides of the hole to the bottom. There the ant lion grabs it. You may find these little pits in a group or *colony* in sandy ground. If you poke carefully with a stick, the ant lion may come rushing out.

People like to call ant lions doodle bugs. There is a little song that goes: "Doodle bug, doodle bug, tell me what I want to know." If the doodle bug comes out of its hole, it is supposed to be telling.

Grasshoppers and Crickets

One of the easiest insects to catch is the grasshopper. If you walk in a meadow or in the grass along the roadside, you may see little bugs jumping away from your feet. These are young grasshoppers. If they have wings and fly, they are adult grasshoppers. Then they are harder to catch!

Very little grasshoppers have no wings at all. You can see the wings beginning to grow as they get bigger. Grasshoppers can be green or brown or gray with spots, and they can have beautifully colored wings.

There are many kinds of grasshoppers. Those with short antennae are called short-horn grasshoppers. Long-horn grasshoppers, whose antennae are nearly as long as their bodies, are also known as katydids. You can hear them sing, "katydid!" on almost any summer night.

Grasshoppers make their songs by rubbing their hind legs against their forewings, the wings on the front of their bodies. They can also rattle their wings in flight. Grasshoppers have their ears in odd places: sometimes on their abdomens or their front legs.

Short-horn grasshopper.

Crickets belong to the same group as grasshoppers. They are fat black or brown insects that jump but seldom fly. The males have a merry song that people have often admired. Crickets make their music by scraping their front wings together. It is often hard to find a cricket because the sound seems to come from all around.

Long-horn grasshopper.

Crickets eat plants, but will also eat meat. They eat almost anything if they are hungry, and can chew up paper, cloth or leather. They can be troublesome pests.

But a plague of grasshoppers can be worse. In places like Africa and some of our midwestern states, grasshoppers sometimes come in great numbers or *swarms*. Millions and millions

Swarm of grasshoppers on airfield in Nairobi, the capital of Kenya, Africa.

of them eat up farmers' crops and every blade of grass. People fight the grasshoppers with brooms and shovels, then kill them with fire and poison. They even fight them from airplanes. But people still have not won the battle. We cannot save all the farmers' crops from a plague of grasshoppers.

Very Small Bugs

Aphids

Some of the smallest insects are very interesting. Aphids are very little insects that eat by sticking their beaks into a plant's stem and sucking up the juice. They eat in much the same way as you suck soda through a straw.

Aphids like rosebushes and other flower plants. If you look in the garden, you will find some flowers whose stems are covered with tiny black, red, or yellow bugs. Through a magnifying glass you can see that they are aphids. They may seem to be standing on their heads. This is because their beaks are stuck into the plant while they suck the juice.

In the fall, female aphids lay eggs which have been fertilized by the males. Aphids also reproduce in the spring, but in a different way. They give birth to live young, all females, and without the help of a male. Very few animals in the world can do this.

Aphids increase so fast that the plant stem is soon covered with them. This saps the plant's strength and makes the flowers wither. But nature has ways of getting rid of aphids. Birds and ladybugs and wasps like to eat them. Ants and bees

Group of aphids sucking sap.

like aphids also, but in another way. For as aphids suck up plant juices with their beaks, they eliminate a sweet liquid called *honeydew*. Bees and ants collect this honeydew and take it to their nests. Some ants protect aphids from other insects so they can get more honeydew.

Most aphids are wingless. But if they need to move to another plant, they develop wings. Aphids may carry the germs of plant diseases when they move. Sugar cane, clover, beans and tobacco are a few plants that may be killed by these diseases. Farmers must fight aphids all summer, as these tiny insects can do great damage.

Another very small insect is the spittle bug. The young ones protect themselves with a froth of bubbles, which they whip

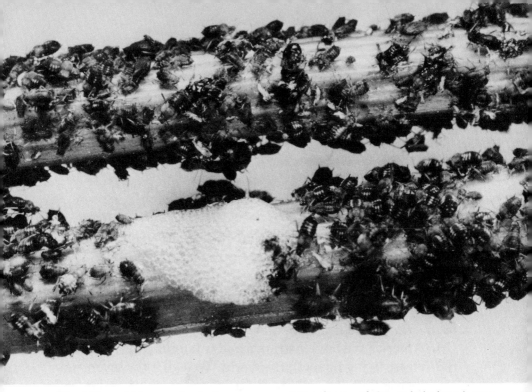

Blackfly aphids on plant stem surround the foam of the spittle bug home.

up with their tails and hide inside. You can sometimes see these frothy balls on the leaves or stems of weeds.

Leafhoppers and Treehoppers

Like aphids, leafhoppers and treehoppers are very small. If you look at them through a magnifying glass, you can see that they have very odd shapes. Their heads may be broad or pointed. Their middle parts may be pushed upwards. Often they look like a thorn on the tree. The adults have wings, but they usually do not fly. They jump instead. They can jump quickly and for long distances.

The Longest-Living Insect

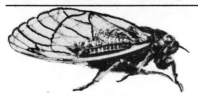

The cicadas (sick-AH-dahs) are closely related to aphids. They also have sharp beaks and eat by sucking the juices from plants and trees.

Cicadas are found all over the world. Most cicadas go through the usual insect life of summer activity and death or *hibernation*, sleep, during the winter.

In America we have a strange and mysterious cicada that is the longest-living insect in the world. We call it the seventeen-year locust, but it is not really a locust, which is a kind of grasshopper. Locusts chew, while cicadas can only suck. Known as *periodical cicadas*, they have learned to live longer by staying underground as juveniles and feeding on the roots of trees. In our southern states, they stay underground for thirteen years. But in the north, they stay for seventeen years.

When the cicadas finally come out of their underground homes, they come in vast numbers. Suddenly, the whole countryside is covered with millions of these insects climbing up out of the ground and into the trees. Here they shed their last skins, spread their wings, and turn into adult insects. They make a terrific noise. All day long a loud humming and buzzing comes from the trees.

It was because of this sudden appearance of millions of insects that the early settlers from Europe called these cicadas locusts. They remembered the plagues of locusts mentioned in the Bible and decided that these insects must be locusts.

People may complain about the noise the cicadas make, but it lasts for only a little more than a month. Then the cicadas die. The noise is the mating call of the males. The females make no noise at all. Their few weeks above ground are spent in finding a mate and in laying eggs. At the end of her abdomen, the female carries a sharp, knifelike organ called an *ovipositor*. With this ovipositor she makes a number of slits on different twigs. She lays between 400 and 600 eggs in the slits. When she is through, she dies.

These slits in tree branches are the only damage cicadas do. The slit causes the twig to break and hang downwards. The

Pencil points to slits made by cicadas.

sap can no longer reach the leaves, so they turn brown. In a cicada year, you can see brown patches all through the woods where the female cicadas have laid their eggs. But the damage will be repaired next year and nobody will know the difference.

Some people think that in this way the cicadas help keep the forests healthy. Only people who grow orchards or fancy trees can find fault with the work of the cicadas. In such cases, some protection can be given to the trees to keep the cicadas away. But as these remarkable insects only appear once in thirteen or seventeen years, it is hardly a serious problem.

Cicadas begin to come out of the ground in May or June. The young cicadas, called *nymphs*, make their way up from underground at night. Then they wait just under the surface until conditions are favorable to come out. They must be sure it is not too cold or stormy. They must be sure no enemies are around who might eat them. Shedding their shells and turning into adult insects is difficult work, and it is hard to protect themselves at that time. Usually, they come out at dusk or during the night to avoid the birds. But if there are a great many, some will still be coming out in the morning.

When they come out of the ground, the cicadas crawl up trees and bushes, up posts and sides of houses. At some point they stop, and a slit appears on the brownish shell at the back of the head. Little by little, the slit lengthens, then the adult insect bursts out. At first, it is all white, with almost no wings. But soon the wings begin to expand and grow larger. The cicada gets darker and darker until, at last, it is all black, with red eyes and orange legs. It stays where it is until its wings are dry and then flies into the nearby trees.

About a week later, mating takes place, and a week after that, the females begin to lay their eggs. By the end of June, their work is done, and most of the adults have disappeared. In mid-July and August, the eggs hatch. The white nymphs are about the size of tiny ants. They are very lively and lose no time in falling to the ground and digging their way into the soil. There, deep in the ground, each nymph makes itself a little cell close to the roots of a tree, sinking its sharp beak into a root and drinking the sap. The nymph sheds its skin five times during its life underground. And as it grows, it enlarges its home. It lives like this for many years, until the magic moment when its instincts say the time has come to leave its underground life and dig its way out into the world of air and sunlight.

Dragonflies

Insects are some of the best fliers in the world. They were the first living things to take to the air. Among the oldest and strongest fliers are the dragonflies. Those early dragonflies had wingspreads of two feet! Today, dragonfly wings are only two to three inches across, although they can reach seven inches in tropical lands.

Dragonflies must live near water. They lay their eggs on water plants. Some drop their eggs right into the water. Damselflies, which are a small kind of dragonfly, make little slits in the stems of water plants. Then they lay their eggs in these slits.

When the eggs hatch, the babies, or nymphs, live in the water. They eat little insects and water animals. Some can even catch small fish. They eat and grow and shed their skins and grow some more. They may live in the water for up to three years. Then they shed their skins for the last time and come out as winged dragonflies. They climb up the stem of a plant, where they come out of their shell, and spread their wings and fly away.

The beautiful dragonfly.

You can easily tell the difference between dragonflies and damselflies. Dragonflies are bigger, and they alight with their wings spread out. The smaller damselflies always fold their wings when they settle down.

Dragonflies may look big and scary, but they cannot hurt you. They have no stinger and will not bite you. But they do bite other insects. Very useful creatures, they catch and eat many flies and gnats and mosquitoes. They are good to have around.

The dragonfly nymph sheds its shell for the last time and becomes a full-fledged dragonfly.

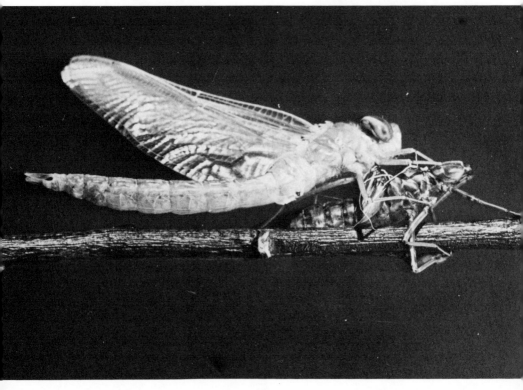

Moths and Butterflies

Moths and butterflies are the most beautiful of all insects. They can be very small or very large. They can have bright, colorful wings or dull, dark wings. They can sit on a tree and look just like the bark. They can move their wings and surprise you with a flash of red or orange from underneath.

How do you know if it is a butterfly or a moth? The first rule for telling is that butterflies fly in the daytime, and moths fly at night. But there are some moths that fly in the late afternoon, so that can be confusing. Another way of telling the difference is that butterflies usually fold their wings upright when they rest. Moths rest with their wings spread out. But, again, this is not *always* so. The best way is to look at the antennae. Butterflies have clubbed antennae. Moths have very thin or sometimes feathery antennae.

Butterflies and moths have four stages of growth. First there is the egg. Some eggs are laid separately, some are laid in groups or clusters. When a caterpillar comes out of a single, separate egg, it also spends its life by itself. But caterpillars

The Monarch butterfly below, the Queen butterfly above.

Tiger moth in resting position. You can see why this moth was given its name!

born from clusters of eggs always live in groups after hatching. A group of caterpillars can eat up all the leaves on the branch of the tree on which they live. But nature takes care of such things. Birds eat hundreds of caterpillars. While the little caterpillars are growing and eating the leaves, baby birds are growing in their nests. The mother birds find plenty of caterpillars to feed to their little ones.

A few caterpillars escape the birds. They eat and grow and shed their skins the way all insects do. When they are full grown, they shed for the last time and come out as pupae. Some moth caterpillars weave a cocoon of silk around themselves before they become pupae. Other moth caterpillars burrow into the ground before they change. Butterfly pupae do not have such protections. Butterfly caterpillars hang themselves from a twig when they are ready to change. They hang there, quite naked, until it is time for them to come out as flying insects. This wonderful change, from crawling caterpillar to flying butterfly or moth, is called *metamorphosis.*

Each kind of butterfly or moth has its own special kind of food plant. Some eat several kinds of plants and some only one. The monarch butterfly eats only milkweed. The luna moth eats the leaves of several different forest trees. If you give them anything else, they will not eat it. They will starve to death. Each mother moth or butterfly knows the right plant for her caterpillars. It is the one she herself ate as a caterpillar. She will lay her eggs only on that plant.

Lackey moth, laying eggs.

Full-grown caterpillar larva.

Monarch larva ready
to pupate on milk-
weed plant.

This group of Bulls-eye moth caterpillars are imiating a flower. This is nature's way of helping protect them from being eaten.

Caterpillars have mouths that chew. They eat lots and lots of leaves. One kind of caterpillar even eats an insect known as plant lice. When caterpillars have finished growing and become butterflies and moths, they cannot chew anymore. Instead, they have long tongues and live by sucking up the *nectar*, the sweet juice deep inside flowers, and other liquids. A few of the largest moths do not eat at all. They live only a short time. They mate and lay their eggs, then they die.

Butterflies and moths give beauty to our gardens and forests. They are also useful insects. Many carry pollen, the male seed, from flower to flower. Without this help, the male and female plants would not be brought together. There would be no fruits and no new plants.

We get silk from the cocoon of the caterpillar of a small moth. We call it a silkworm. There is a story that a Chinese empress watched the moths in her garden and learned the secret of the silken cocoon. But that was so long ago that nobody can be sure. Anyway, the Chinese learned how to take silk from the silkworm's cocoon and spin it into thread. They have been raising silkworms for thousands of years. The moths have lived in cages so long that now they cannot fly.

A few butterflies and moths can be harmful pests. Usually they are not native to our country but have come from abroad. One such is known as the cabbage white, which came from Europe with the early settlers. Its caterpillars can be very destructive to crops. They eat lettuce and cabbage and other vegetables.

Another caterpillar, that of the gypsy moth, also came from Europe. It can destroy acres of forest trees. Every year some foresters want to spray the trees to protect them from the gypsy moth. But the spray kills other insects, and frogs and birds. The spray is so harsh it can spoil the paint on automobiles and the laundry hanging on the line. Since people don't like this, there is usually an argument with foresters about spraying.

Flies

A fly is a fly, you may think. But to scientists a fly is a two-winged insect. There are many kinds of flies in the world. Mosquitoes are also put in the fly group. This seems right, since both these insects make trouble for us.

Mosquitoes

To you, mosquitoes may seem to be the worst because their bite is so disagreeable. A mosquito bite can itch and sting for some time. Actually, the mosquito does not sting. It inserts its beak through your skin and sucks up blood. It is only the female mosquito that drinks your blood and makes the whining sound that warns you of her presence. The male does not have a strong enough beak to pierce your skin. He lives on plant juices instead.

Mosquitoes lay their eggs in water, usually in *stagnant* ponds, where the water is still and does not run off, or any little pool where water collects. The young, called *wrigglers,* live in the water until they are full grown. Then they change into pupae called *tumblers.* Tumblers continue to live in water, but only for a few days. Then the winged insects come out.

36

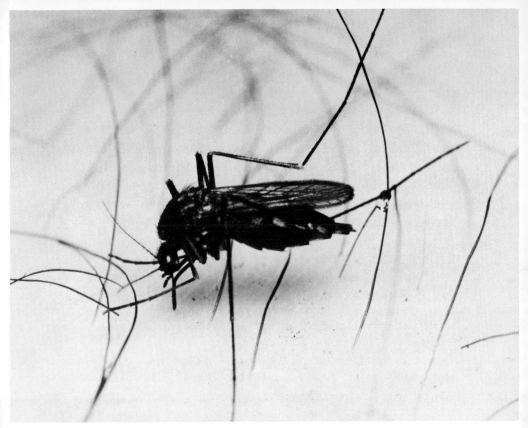

Female mosquito of the family called *Culex.*

Mosquitoes have learned to live in all parts of the world, from the hot tropics to the cold arctic. They can be dangerous, because some mosquitoes carry diseases. Malaria and yellow fever are two diseases we can get from a mosquito bite. But the mosquitoes who carry these diseases live mostly in tropical climates.

To fight these diseases, waters where the mosquito eggs and young are found are sprayed. Water from stagnant ponds is drained. New ways of killing mosquitoes are being invented all the time. One uses a sound like the female's song. This lures the males to their deaths on electric screens. Without males to fertilize the eggs, it is hoped that there will soon be fewer mosquitoes.

Other Flies

There are horseflies that have a nasty bite. There are robber flies that eat other insects, especially bees, and so are

Horsefly.

disliked by beekeepers. There are fruitflies, which reproduce so rapidly that they are helpful to scientists who study heredity.

The fly you know best is the housefly. Houseflies like the warmth of our houses and the food we eat. They also like to eat any dead and dirty thing they find outdoors. Flies like manure, garbage, and dirty water, all filled with disease germs. The fly brings those germs to the food on our table, spreading disease. Thirty or forty diseases are carried by the housefly. If you want to stay well and strong, keep flies out of your house. Screens on doors and windows help. If flies get in, kill them with a fly swatter or insect spray. But always be careful not to spray near food. What kills the fly can also make you sick.

Some flies can fool you. They are called hoverflies. They don't look like flies at all. They look like bees or wasps. The hoverflies have copied the bright yellow, orange, or red markings of bees and wasps. But they do not have a sting. How can you tell the difference between them? Bees have four wings and hoverflies have only two. If you can be sure that the insect has only two wings, you are safe. It cannot sting. But that is a hard thing to see when the insect is hovering over a flower. Hoverflies also copy bees by buzzing or humming as they hover. This buzzing does not come from their wings but from the *thorax*, the chest. However, bees stop buzzing when they settle on a flower. Hoverflies keep right on making noise.

Hoverflies are beautiful, and very useful. Next to bees, they

This hoverfly, on a garden flower, looks like a bee.

are the best pollinators, carrying the male pollen to the female flowers. Hoverflies live entirely on the nectar of flowers. Their wings go very fast and they seem to stand still in the air. All this takes a great deal of energy, and nectar does not supply as much energy as the meat the hoverflies' relatives eat. The hoverfly solves this problem by eating lots of meat during childhood. Each species has a different way of feeding its young, but most supply their larvae with other insects as food.

Some hoverfly larvae eat aphids, and others eat the larvae of ants and bees. They are storing up energy so that when they change into flies they can hover in the sunlight over our flowers. And this helps to bring a good crop to our orchards and gardens.

The drone fly, which looks almost exactly like a male bee, lays its eggs in stagnant pools. The larvae walk along the bottom, eating tiny forms of life they find there. But they need air to breathe. So they use their tails to reach the air above. They can make their tails as short or as long as needed.

Beetles

There are 277,000 kinds of beetles in the world and more are being found all the time. They are the largest group of insects.

Beetles have four wings, but the front pair have become hard shells. These cover and protect the rear wings, with which the insect flies.

Ladybirds

A favorite beetle is the ladybird beetle or ladybug. It is small and round, red or orange in color, with two or more black spots on its outer wings. A well-known song says:

> Ladybird, ladybird,
>   Fly away home.
> Your house is on fire
>   And your children will burn.

If you say this to a ladybird beetle on your open hand, it is supposed to fly away.

Ladybird beetles.

Whether it does so or not, ladybird beetles are good to have in the garden. They eat lots of aphids and other insect pests. They are so useful that farmers pay to have them put in their fields and orchards. It takes about three thousand beetles to protect an acre of fruit trees.

Some people make a business of searching for ladybirds. They dig them up and sell them to the farmers. They are not too hard to find, for ladybird beetles spend the winter in great masses, crowded together under rocks and fallen trees.

The Fun Bug

Perhaps the insect that is the most fun is the firefly. In Japan there is a firefly festival. The firefly is not really a fly, but a beetle. It can make flashes of light with its tail. Lights that people make give off heat. But the firefly makes cold light. We are still trying to learn how!

There are many different kinds of fireflies. Some kinds have no wings and cannot fly. They are sometimes called glowworms. Female glowworms flash their lights in the grass to attract males. Eggs are laid upon the ground, and the young can flash their lights even before hatching. They may take from one to two years to grow into a winged, adult form.

Everyone loves to see the little firefly lights flashing on and off across the lawns and fields. In the tropics there are trees where swarms of fireflies gather. This makes the tree look like a Christmas tree whose lights are set to go off and on.

Each kind of firefly has its own special signal so that it will be sure to find the right mate. But among our American fireflies, there is one female that fakes another species' flash. When a male responds to this flash, he is grabbed and eaten.

The difference in flashes depends on the length of time between the male's flash and the female's answering flash. So if you take a flashlight into the field at night and are able to copy the female's signal, you may make the male firefly come to you. You may like to catch a few and put them in a glass jar. They will light up for you there and you can watch them close at hand.

The Monster Insect

If you are looking for insects late in summer, the largest one you are likely to see is the adult praying mantis. If you see two, they are called praying mantids. At first sight you may find a praying mantis frightening.

The praying mantis is the monster of the insect world. Our native mantis is medium-sized. The Chinese and the European mantids have come to this country and both are very large. But they are quite harmless to us. It is a helpful creature to have in the garden, for it eats large numbers of insect pests.

Even though it is big, the praying mantis is not always easy to see. It is green or light brown in color and sits so quietly that it looks like a leaf. Hidden like this, it waits for some insect to come near, then reaches out and grabs the victim with its forelegs. These have a row of spines that close like a jaw upon the captive so that it cannot get away. The mantis then slowly eats its meal.

Praying mantis about to strike at an ant.

The praying mantis is the only insect that can turn its head all the way around and see in all directions. It seems to be afraid of nothing and will fight animals much bigger than itself.

After mating, the female often eats the male. The eggs of the praying mantis are laid in a mass of froth made by the mother mantis. This froth dries to make a strong, hard egg

Caught!

case. The case protects the eggs through the winter. In the spring, tiny mantids hatch. It takes them all summer to grow to adult size.

In captivity, mantids eat one another, and you cannot keep more than one mantis in a cage. In spite of this, they make interesting pets.

The Social Insects

The most interesting insects are called the social insects. This is because they all work together to build their nests, get their food, and defend themselves. Some bees and wasps and all the ants and termites are social insects. These insects build nests with many rooms and runways. In some ways, these are like the cities we build. Bees, ants and wasps do not think and learn as we do. But they know how to build wonderful cities.

Almost all the ants and bees that you see running and flying about are females. We call them workers, for they do all the work. They are not *fertile* females, females that have mated with a male and lay eggs.

There is usually one larger female that is fertile. We call this large female the queen. But she does not rule the workers. All she does is lay eggs. She rarely leaves the nest, and the workers feed and care for her.

Ants

Ants build their nests, or cities, in the ground or in wood. Some ants in the tropics build nests of leaves up in the trees. They have remarkable ways of building. No matter what the weather is outside, the ants' nests are just right inside. They

These are red ants. The queen in the center is surrounded by workers—the larvae are underneath.

can keep their nests warm enough and dry enough and cool enough.

In some rooms of the nest are piles of eggs. The workers bring them here as fast as the queen lays them. They turn them over and lick them to keep them clean. In other rooms are the larvae that have hatched from the eggs. The workers feed the larvae. They also move them from one part of the nest to another as the sun makes the nest warmer or as night makes it cooler. In still other rooms are the pupae. This is the third stage of growing, when the young ant rests before it changes into an adult ant. The worker ants care for the pupae, too, and move them around in the nest. Then they help young ants to come out when they are ready to emerge.

Winged ant.

Ants usually work first as nurses, caring for the eggs and the larvae and the pupae and feeding the queen. Later they go outside and begin looking for food. Then they are called foragers. They also help to build and repair the nest.

Ants eat many different kinds of food. Some eat more variety than others. There are ants that eat seeds of plants but do not care for meat. Others may not care for seeds and so eat all kinds of insects. They cut up and carry home dead insects that they find or kill. An ant can carry a load much bigger than itself.

Ants are very fond of sweets. They collect the sap from trees when it oozes out in the spring. They also collect drops of honeydew from aphids. Some ants have groups of aphids they tend every day. For this reason, aphids have been called ants' cows. Some ants are even said to build shelters over their aphids. Other ants take aphids into their nests to care for. They place the aphids on the underground roots of plants so they can feed.

Other kinds of ants have become gardeners, cutting leaves from the trees and carrying them home to their nests. The leaves are chewed up by the ants and placed in the underground rooms. The leaves make a rich garden bed in which the ants grow a kind of fungus. The ants eat this fungus, which is a kind found only in ant nests. When a young queen flies to start a new ant city, she carries a tiny bit of the fungus with her.

Building the nest, taking care of the brood, feeding the queen and the young, all take a lot of work. Ant cities have thousands of workers.

Ants have wars with other ant cities. It has been said that ants and human beings are the only animals that make war on their own kind. For this reason, there are ant guards for the nests. Some have very big jaws and stand around like soldiers watching for the enemy. Others have strange, round heads that are the same size as the entrance to the nest. When the guard puts its head in the entry hole, nothing can get in or out.

When ants make war, a great stream of them leave the nest and go to raid a nearby colony of another species. The ants rush into this nest, grab the larvae and pupae, and carry them back to their own nest. The victims try to save their brood. But much of it is carried off by the raiders. The young ants grow up to be slave workers in the new nest. Many ants may be killed in battle.

Sometime you may happen upon an ant war. See if you can learn what is going on. Hundreds of ants will be rushing about. Some will be carrying little white things. These are the pupae and larvae they are stealing. A couple of scientists were once several hours late to a party because they came upon an ant war. Nothing could drag them away!

At certain times of the year there will be ants with wings in the nest. These are the young males and females. When the weather is just right, the workers let them out. Then they fly off to mate and start new nests. But very few will do so, because most will be killed. Animals, birds and other insects like to eat flying ants. In some parts of the world, people do, too!

Ants live in all parts of the world except the frozen regions. They can live in dry deserts and in the hot tropics and in everybody's garden.

Bees

Certain kinds of bees and wasps live in much the same way as ants. The well-known bee that builds a city is the honeybee. Bees were living this way and making honey long before there were human beings. Humans learned early to like the taste of honey, and put the bees to work for us. Farmers have been making hives for bee breeding for thousands of years. Now it has become a big business and a science.

Bees do not take honey from a flower, they take nectar. The bees collect the nectar and take it back to the hive. There they store it in their six-sided cells and make it into honey. They do this by fanning the nectar with their wings so that the moisture is drawn out. Only the thick honey remains. The workers feed honey to the queen bee, the larvae, the male drones and each other.

More important than the honey you like to eat is the fact that bees take pollen from flower to flower. The powdery pollen clings to their legs and bodies as they enter and leave the flower in their search for nectar. Without bees, many plants would not bloom or grow. We would have no apples, no berries, no clover. For this reason, farmers pay to have beekeepers bring hives to their fields. Many beekeepers spend the summer moving their bees in trucks from farm to farm, even from state to state. If the truck has an accident, there is great trouble on the highway!

Bee cities are different from ant cities. In the wild, bee cities are built in a hollow tree. On farms, the bees are kept in a round or square box they build in. The box has a little hole to go in and out, and contains frames within which the bees build their combs of wax. They build hundreds of little cells with the wax, which comes from their bodies. All the cells have six sides, and all fit exactly together.

In some cells of the hive, the queen bee lays her eggs, one egg to a cell. The baby bee that comes out of the egg has no legs and cannot wiggle around. It stays in the cell while it eats and grows and changes. It spins a cocoon while still in the cell and becomes a pupa. Later it comes out as an adult bee and must begin to work. It works hard all its life, as a nurse, taking care of the queen, helping to build the hive. It fans its wings to keep the hive cool and dry, flies to collect nectar from flowers, and sometimes fights to defend its home. Finally, it dies. Worker bees live only a few weeks in the summer. The queen bee can live for years.

The queen honeybee (center) is laying eggs, with the workers attending her.

In addition to honey, the bees make a special food called royal jelly for their babies. Ordinary bee babies are fed this for the first three days of their lives, after which they are given honey. When a new queen is needed, the workers build several special, larger cells. The eggs the queen lays in them are the same as the eggs that make workers, but these babies are fed royal jelly until they pupate. When they emerge, they are queen bees, ready to mate and lay eggs for the rest of their long lives. They are also ready to fight, and the first queen to emerge destroys all the others.

Soon after winning the battle, the new queen flies out of the hive to find a mate. This is called the *nuptial flight,* and all the male bees, called *drones,* that have been sitting around the hive follow her. Other drones from nearby hives fly after her, too. Higher and faster she flies, till one drone catches and mates with her. After mating, he dies, leaving his *sperm* seed inside her to fertilize the many, many eggs that she will lay.

The queen returns to the hive, followed by the unsuccessful drones. There the workers welcome her. They feed her and clean her and care for her the rest of her life. But they soon stop feeding the drones. Their job is done, and they are only more mouths to feed. Soon the workers will not let them into the hive. Then the drones die of cold and hunger in the approaching winter.

In the cold months, the rest of the bees huddle together in a tight swarm inside the hive. Sometimes, if they are on a farm, they eat a bit of honey or sugar water given them by the farmer. Mostly they sleep. The queen is in the middle of the swarm and the workers move about from the outer to the inner part so that all will be warmed.

Wasps

There are two types of social wasps. One is the yellow jacket, which builds its nest in the ground. The other is the hornet, which builds a nest that hangs in a tree and looks like a football. These nests do not last more than one summer. When cold weather comes, all the workers die and the nests fall apart. Only the new fertile queens are left. The queens find safe places to sleep through the winter. In spring they each start a new nest which their many offspring build into a big city during the summer. By fall each will have thousands of workers.

A wasp's life is much like a bee's life, but there are differences. The chief difference is that the bee feeds its babies on honey and pollen from flowers, and the wasp feeds its babies on meat—other insects.

The wasp's city is also different from the bee's. It is not built of wax but of paper. You may see a wasp sitting on a fence post. It is not just sitting there. It is probably chewing out a tiny bit of wood which it will make into paper for its nest. Also, the wasp builds its nest upside down. Both the outdoor and underground nests hang from a branch or rock. The cells are also upside down. The egg is stuck inside the cell and the little larva holds onto the cell and hangs upside down.

Wasps do not give us honey to eat or wax to use. They are pests when they steal our food at a picnic and then sting us when we object. But they are useful nevertheless. They pollinate many plants and flowers. And they eat many other insects that would cause us a great deal of trouble if there were no wasps around to kill them.

Wasp and nest.

Common wasps'
nest, covering
removed to show
combs inside.

How to Watch and Collect Insects

How many insects can you see on a day in the country? A lot, if you know how to look. Insects hide themselves well. Some hide in the grass. Some hide under stones. Some hide under the bark of trees. Catching them is not always easy.

How can you have fun with them when you catch them? Grasshoppers and crickets make nice pets for a few days and are easy to feed, as they eat any type of vegetable. The Chinese and Japanese make little cages for crickets and hang them in their houses to hear them sing. They also have "cricket fights." Cricket fans watch the fights and make bets. In the old days, a good fighting cricket was worth a lot of money.

Many people make a hobby of collecting dead insects. To do this, you need a *killing jar* and special boxes in which to keep your specimens. You must have little pins to pin the specimens in the box. If you collect butterflies and moths, you must learn the art of spreading and mounting them.

It is easier and perhaps more interesting to keep one or two insects alive and watch them grow and see what they do. All you need is a glass or plastic jar with a good lid or a cover of netting. The netting can be held in place with an elastic band.

Prickly stick insect is well hidden in its natural surroundings.

If you use a lid, it is not necessary to make holes for air. Insects do not require as much air as would larger animals.

You will need a long-handled net if you go after butterflies or water beetles. And you must be sure you know what your insect eats, or you will not be able to keep it alive. Grasshoppers are easily fed with grass or lettuce. The praying mantis must have flies or other insects. The mantis will sometimes also eat chopped meat, but you must wiggle the meat to make it seem alive. The mantis will also drink water out of a spoon.

Butterflies and moths are fun to watch. The best way is to watch the adult grow from a caterpillar. But you must be sure to have the right plant to feed it. Often the plant you find it on is what it eats. Some caterpillars, like the woolly bear caterpillar, will eat lettuce. Keep your caterpillar in the jar and be sure it always has fresh leaves. Keep the jar clean of dead leaves and other dirt. If you watch closely, you can see it

These are the things the author used for collecting and rearing insects.

shed its skin as it grows. You can see it change into a pupa. When ready to change, caterpillars stop eating and crawl about, looking for the best place to pupate. It is good to have a stick in the cage for them to hang from. When satisfied with a place, they fasten themselves to it. About two weeks later, you can expect the butterfly to come out. But if it is late summer, the butterfly may not come out until the next spring. It will sleep all winter. At this time you should put it in a cool place. Heat will make it come out too soon.

Some people make a hobby of raising monarch butterflies. They take part in the international tagging program of these remarkable insects. Monarch butterflies migrate like the birds. Every spring they fly north from their winter homes in Mexico and southern California. They fly thousands of miles, often as far as Canada. Along the way, the females lay their eggs on milkweed plants. When the caterpillars have become butterflies—in about a month—they also fly farther north. In the fall, great swarms of monarchs fly south again to spend the winter, hanging in groups from the branches of trees and feeding from the flowers on sunny days.

For many years, a scientist in Toronto, Canada, has conducted a tagging program for monarchs. People all over the country help him. Some raise monarchs, and the scientist sends them little tags to fasten on the wings before setting the butterflies free. Other people watch for the monarchs. When they find one with a tag on its wing, they send it to the scientist in Toronto. He can then tell how far the butterfly flew

Painted Lady butterfly emerging from chrysalis.

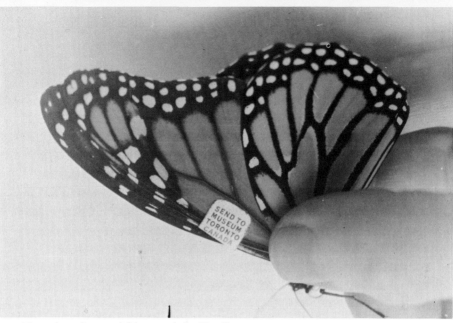
Here is a tagged Monarch butterfly.

and where it came from. It is exciting to have one of the butterflies you raised found and returned, and to know where it was going on its long migration.

Although social insects lead such interesting lives, watching them is not easy. People who study wasps and bees are quite apt to be stung. And ant nests are usually far underground.

It is possible to build an artificial nest for ants, with glass sides so that you can watch them as they go about their daily lives. Special stores even sell these nests with ants living in them. These nests are divided into two parts. One is for the ant city and the other is the foraging area. Here their food, usually sugar water, is put. Through the glass walls you can watch the busy lives of the ants.

Whatever insect you decide to watch, if you look carefully, you may discover something new about its behavior that nobody knew before!

Index

Africa, 17
America, 22
antennae, 9, 15, 29
ant lion, 14
ants, 12, 14, 19, 20, 25, 41, 48-52, 63
aphids, 19-20, 21, 22, 41, 43, 50

beekeepers, 39, 53
bees, 12, 19, 20, 38, 39, 41, 48, 52-55, 63
beetles, 42-43, 44
Bible, locusts mentioned in, 23
butterflies, 9, 12, 29-35, 58, 59, 60, 63; monarch, 31, 61

Canada, 61
caterpillars, 9, 12, 29, 31, 34, 35, 61; wooly bear, 60
cicadas, 22-25; periodical, 22
cocoon, 31, 35, 53
"cricket fights," 58
crickets, 15-18, 58

damselflies, 26, 28
doodle bug. See ant lion
dragonflies, 26-28

Europe, 23, 35

fireflies, 44
flies, 28, 36-41; drone, 41; fruit, 39; horse, 38; house, 39; hover, 39-41; robber, 38

glowworms, 44
gnats, 28
grasshopper, 15-18, 22, 58, 59; long-horn, 15; short-horn, 15

hibernation, 22
honey, 52, 53, 54, 55, 56
honeydew, 20, 50
hornet, 55

Japan, 44

katydids, 15

killing jar, 58

ladybird beetles (ladybugs), 19, 42-43
larvae, 12, 40, 41, 49, 50, 51, 52
leafhoppers, 21
locusts, 22

malaria, 37
metamorphosis, 31
Mexico, 61
mosquitoes, 28, 36-38
moths, 9, 12, 29-35, 58, 60; luna, 31, gypsy, 35

nectar, 34, 40, 52, 53
nuptial flight, 54
nymphs, 24, 25, 26

ovipositor, 23

plant lice, 34
pollen, 35, 40, 53, 56
praying mantis, 45-47, 59
pupae, 12, 31, 36, 49, 50, 51

royal jelly, 54

seventeen-year locust. See cicadas, periodical
silk, 35
silkworm, 35
social insects, 48-57, 63
spittle bug, 20
swarms, 17

termites, 48
thorax, 39
treehoppers, 21
tumblers, 36

wasps, 19, 39, 48, 52, 55-57, 63
water beetles, 59
wrigglers, 36

yellow fever, 37
yellow jackets, 55